HOW TO RESEARCH HISTORIC OCCUPATIONS

A GUIDE FOR FAMILY HISTORY RESEARCHERS

ANDREW CHAPMAN

H
heritagehunter

ISBN 9781905315666 (print)

ISBN 9781905315678 (ebook)

H heritagehunter

CONTENTS

INTRODUCTION

Whether we like it or not, we are all defined, to some degree, by our occupations. If anything, it was all the more so for our ancestors. There was little time for discussion of work–life balance, productivity tools or early retirement – for most people in ordinary circumstances, they would start work at a young age, have few days off, and keep going until they died or hit their dotage. Even the introduction of compulsory education for children aged between five and ten, with the Elementary Education Acts of 1870 and 1880, was widely resented as it took children away from contributing to the family income. The long summer holidays that today's parents similarly resent is a vestigial legacy of the compromise reached to allow children to help with the harvest.

Occupations have inevitably been influenced by changes in society and technology. The obvious example is the impact of the Industrial Revolution from the late 18th century onwards. At the start of the 19th century, around three-quarters of the working population were involved in agriculture and only a quarter in urban industry – less than a century later, the proportions had reversed.

This not only meant that your ancestor may have changed their trade, but also that they migrated within the UK. Census data shows urban populations exploding as people flocked in search of work, although this often meant cramped and insanitary conditions, affecting their health too. And some trades saw migration anyway – there have always been people relocating in search of a better life or more available employment. Some trades are strongly associated with particular regions nonetheless – hence Manchester's reputation as 'Cottonopolis', the prevalence of framework knitting in Nottinghamshire and Leicestershire, or even more specific local expertise such as rope-making in Bridport

OCCUPATIONAL RECORDS

With an almost endless range of different trades practised by people down the ages, tracking down occupational records can be complicated. Many businesses have kept records, and some trades faced specific bureaucracy that means a paper trail can be followed; but others have been lost to obscurity.

However, there are also several major categories of record which can help to shed light on your forebears' work history. One is the census, of course, which from 1841 onwards listed details of individuals' trades and, from 1891, whether they were employed, self-employed or an employer themselves. Birth, marriage and death certificates, going back to 1837 for England and Wales and 1855 for Scotland, can often provide occupational clues, too. Birth certificates will reveal the father's occupation (and the mother's from 1894); marriage records likewise, as well as the professions of the marrying pair. Death certificates also reveal the individual's trade, if they were still working – and, of course, the cause of death might have been related to their work. Going back through time, parish records often record occupation (in baptisms, for the father, usually after 1812), but by no means always.

Apprenticeship records in some cases date back to the 13th century when the trade guild system began. From 1563, it actually became illegal to enter a trade without undertaking an apprenticeship – this usually began between the ages of 10 and 14, and typically lasted for seven years. Older apprenticeship records can sometimes be found in county record offices or transcribed in the Society of Genealogists' library in London; the SoG also has some digitised within its SoG Data Online collections, which are available to members via www.sog.org.uk. You will more likely be in luck for the period 1710—1811, when stamp duty was payable on apprenticeship indentures – this left a paper trail, the records of which are available at all three of the main data websites, TheGenealogist, Ancestry and Findmypast. TheGenealogist also has merchant navy apprenticeship records (1824–1910); Ancestry has regional collections for Dorset and West Yorkshire; and Findmypast also has a collection of London apprenticeship abstracts from 1442 to 1850 – and if your research encompasses ancestors in the capital, it's also worth looking at www.londonlives.org. And remember: these records will typically list both the apprentice and their master, so you might find forebears who were new to the trade, or indeed those who were experienced.

The Modern Records Centre

An essential resource for much occupational research is the Modern Records Centre at the University of Warwick (www.warwick.ac.uk/services/library/mrc/). Founded in 1973, this is the main British repository for national archives of trade unions and employers' organisations, and you can visit its centre on weekdays (check the website for up-to-date opening times). The MRC also has many smaller collections relating to particular trades compiled by individuals. For an overview of its offerings, see www.warwick.ac.uk/services/library/mrc/holdings/main_archives/, plus the A-Z list of occupations at www.warwick.ac.uk/services/library/mrc/explorefurther/subject_guides/family_history.

DIRECTORIES & NEWSPAPERS

Trade directories are an obvious resource, and again Ancestry, Findmypast and TheGenealogist all have large and growing collections which have been digitised. The first ones appeared in the 18th century, although they were only really common from the mid-19th century onwards. You can also find more for England and Wales within the University of Leicester's collection (see below), for Scotland at https://digital.nls.uk/directories/ and for Northern Ireland at www.nidirect.gov.uk/information-and-services/search-archives-online/street-directories.

Websites for trade directories

Historical Directories of England & Wales

This website has changed its URL over the years but the current one is below. This project is hosted by the University of Leicester and has many directories dating from the 1760s to the 1910s. Note that the collection is now also available within Ancestry.

https://le.ac.uk/library/special-collections/explore/historical-directories

Scottish Post Office Directories

This collection, compiled by the National Library of Scotland, offers more than 700 digitised directories covering most of Scotland and dating from 1773 to 1911, all for free. The directories can be searched by place, year and name.

https://digital.nls.uk/directories/

Irish Directory Database

Shane Wilson and Joe Buggy have compiled this useful database which has links to more than 1000 historic trade directories for Ireland – some of those are free online, others at paid-for sites or, indeed, on CD (the database indicates which have to be paid for).

www.swilson.info/dirdb.php

If you're lucky to be able to push your ancestry back to pre-Tudor times, your ancestor may have been a member of a trade guild or London livery company. Local record offices sometimes have holdings for the former, and the latter all have archives (usually at London's Guildhall Library). See also the records at the Records of London's Livery Companies Online (www.londonroll.org) which cover the period from 1400 to 1900. Wills, from that era until the present day, can also provide clues or direct references to an individual's occupation, the tools of their trade, their co-workers and so on.

Returning to the last 200 years, newspapers can also reveal occupational titbits – not just reports of, say, occupational awards your ancestor may have won or encounters with the law, but also reports of industrial accidents. Further, as time went on advertisements became more common in newspapers and you might find a forebear's shop or other service featured in one. The British Newspaper Archive (www.britishnewspaperarchive.co.uk) is a great starting point.

There have been more than 5,000 trade unions since they began to flourish in the early 19th century. The website www.unionancestors.co.uk has a variety of useful information on the subject, as well as a list of known trade unions by name, which could help you track down their records elsewhere, most likely at the Modern Records Centre (see page 4).

Larger businesses will have kept their own records – the Postal Museum Archive, for example, will help you find records of postal workers (see www.postalmuseum.org/visit/the-archive/); BT has archives going back to 1846 (www.bt.com/about/bt/our-history/bt-archives); and The National Archives catalogue provides information about many business-specific archives around England and Wales.

One type of record which you might not have come across is fire insurance certificates – businesses were required to have them and they can provide useful information about a business, its premises and the people involved. These mainly date from the 18th century onwards and there are some online at TNA – see www.genguide.co.uk/source/fire-insurance-registers-plans-and-maps/89/ for details of the resources available.

Women and children

We joke today, perhaps, about sending our kids 'down the mines' or 'up the chimneys', but child labour was a fact of life before the 20th century. Children did indeed go down the mines, as the famous Commissioners' Report of Children's Employment from 1842 attests (see www.balmaiden.co.uk/1842.htm). This led to the Mines Act of 1842, which banned children under ten from working in the mines, and more legislation eventually came, such as the Chimney Sweepers Acts of 1840 and 1875, and the advent of compulsory education.

The 1841 census occupations abstract distinguished between workers under 20 or 20 and over. The top five occupations for under 20s (of either sex) were, in decreasing order: domestic servant, agricultural labourer, cotton worker, general labourer and coal miner.

The top five occupations for adult women in the same year, meanwhile, were, in descending order: domestic servant, dressmaker/milliner, cotton worker, laundrykeeper/washerwoman and agricultural labourer. Looking at the 1841 data, we can see that women were involved in far more trades than we might have assumed – more than 640 of the 877 occupations listed had at least some women doing them, and of the 88 occupations with at least 10,000 people recorded, around half of them had at least 1000 women working in them. The moral of the story is that, although many women would have looked after children, and they dominated domestic service and some textile work, you should not assume your female ancestors couldn't have had some employment in many other trades.

Typically, it is easier to follow middle-class or professional ancestors, as clerical work inherently left more paperwork, as did occupations that required qualifications such as the law, medicine or the clergy. Nevertheless, if your forebears were typically manual workers, don't despair! There are many surviving factory records, trade union lists, registers of social clubs and so on which can be tracked down – county record offices or TNA's Discovery catalogue will be good starting points. The Modern Records Centre is a key place to know about – see the box. Other relevant archives can be found at the People's History Museum in Manchester (https://phm.org.uk/collection-search/) and the Museum of Rural Life in Reading (merl.reading.ac.uk). The National Museum Wales's library has many holdings relating to work in Wales, such as apprenticeship indentures and craftsmen's account books – see https://museum.wales/curatorial/social-cultural-history/archives/.

Above all, researching your ancestors' occupations is a rewarding activity – it brings them more vividly to life, and will help you understand their status, location and some of the decisions they will have faced in their lives, just as our jobs affect us today.

Scottish occupations

Much of the information on these pages pertains to Scotland as much as it does England and Wales. A look at the occupational abstract for 1841 shows that the top 20 occupations across the whole working population were mostly very similar. Notably higher up the charts in Scotland were fishermen and women, seamstresses, on shore seamen and carriers/carters; and notably lower were factory workers, silk, lace and worsted workers, and those in pottery manufacture. All of this seems to suggest Scotland was still less industrialised (other than coal mining) than the rest of the UK.

Many Scottish trades had their own organisations, of course, which may well have kept records, and there were differences in the apprenticeship system. There are some useful starting points at www.familysearch.org/wiki/en/Scotland_Occupations, and a list of old Scottish trades at www.scotlandsfamily.com/occupations.htm.

Further resources

Dictionaries of occupational terms: Census enumerators were given a handbook listing the occupational terms they might have encountered. These can still be useful today for understanding the more unusual trades. The particularly comprehensive 1927 Dictionary of Occupational Terms (based on what was used for the 1921 census) has been digitised by Peter Christian and is available for free at http://doot.spub.co.uk. Rodney Hall also maintains a good list of old trades from abactor to zoographer at http://rmhh.co.uk/occup/index.html.

Genuki: One of the unsung heroes of genealogy online is the Genuki portal. Its cornucopia of information includes a very useful page with links to lots of occupation-specific resources – find it at www.genuki.org.uk/big/Occupations.

UKGDL: UKGDL is a portal site which offers many useful lists and directories of relevance to genealogy. It includes an occupational section, which you can browse at http://ukgdl.org.uk/category/occupations or search at http://ukgdl.org.uk/occupations – the database consists of useful links to resources across the internet.

Mailing lists: It can often be of great help to find other researchers with an interest in the same occupation as your ancestor's. The RootsWeb community hosted by Ancestry has more than 80 mailing lists devoted to occupations (although not all of them pertain to the UK). If there's one for your family trade, you can search its archives or simply join in and ask other people on the list for advice. An index of mailing lists is at https://sites.rootsweb.com/~jfuller/gen_mail_occ.html.

FamilySearch Wiki: This huge encyclopedia of genealogical information has a large section on English occupations (and Scottish – see box) at www.familysearch.org/wiki/en/England_Occupations, and a small section for Wales at www.familysearch.org/wiki/en/Wales_Occupations.

THE TOP TRADES

This alphabetical list covers many of the most common occupational fields in the 19th century. More specifically, it has been compiled on the basis of the decennial census reports from 1841 and 1891. A huge challenge for exploring occupational data across time is the changes made to the way the censuses were compiled (a summary is at www.visionofbritain.org.uk/travellers/Cen_Guide/4). The famed surveyor of London poverty, Charles Booth, attempted to marshal this information into a better format, and his work was continued by Professor Alan Armstrong in the 1970s (see *Nineteenth-century Society* (Cambridge University Press, 1972)). The list below uses Armstrong's classification for 1841-1891 as a basis for identifying the top trades by number of people employed for England and Wales, with some categories combined for clarity.

The trades listed here actually account for more than 90 per cent of the working population in 1841, and more than 82 per cent for 1891 (the lower figure reflects the greater diversity of trades by this time). The figures show the number of workers in thousands.

AGRICULTURAL LABOURERS

1841: 962.1 • 1891: 759.2

In only 50 years, the number of 'ag labs', the stalwarts of pre-industrial society, had declined more than 20%. Researching these humble toilers can be tricky but glimpses of them and their lives can be caught in local newspapers, Quarter Sessions records, Poor Law records, farmers' diaries, manorial documents (via TNA) and rural life museums (see www.ruralmuseums.org.uk).

Useful resources:

- WALLER, Ian. 2014. My Ancestor Was an Agricultural Labourer. Society of Genealogists
- HANDFORD, K. 2011. The agricultural labourer in 19th century England. Grosvenor House
- GREEN, F.E. 1920. A history of the English agricultural labourer
- HAMMOND, J.L. & HAMMOND, Barbara. 1911. The Village Labourer 1760-1832

ARMY OFFICERS & SOLDIERS

1841: 36.6 • 1891: 91.5

The British Army as an organised force dates back to the 17th century, although records are few before the formalisation of service records in the 1760s. The definitive place to start for all British Army records is The National Archives, which has a series of useful research guides. Service, pension and discharge records can be found back to the early 18th century, as well as muster rolls and pay lists. Annual Army Lists from 1754 to 1879 list officers.

Useful resources:

- Numerous TNA guides at http://bit.ly/2KJHjN0
- WATTS, C. & W. 2014. My Ancestor was in the British Army. Society of Genealogists
- JOLLY, E. 2013. My Ancestor was a Woman at War. Society of Genealogists
- FOWLER, Simon. 2017. Tracing Your Army Ancestors - 3rd Edition. Pen & Sword
- INGHAM, Mary. 2012. Tracing Your Service Women Ancestors. Pen & Sword

ARTISTS (PAINTERS, SCULPTORS, ENGRAVERS)

1841; 9.1 • 1891: 12.3

Major galleries maintain databases of established visual artists – places to start include the Tate Archive Collections (www.tate.org.uk/art/archive/collections) and the Royal Academy Archives (www.royalacademy.org.uk/art-artists/search/archives) – the latter has papers back to the mid-18th century. Newspapers often carried reports of exhibitions. The Visual Arts Data Service provides links to numerous collections (www.vads.ac.uk).

Useful resources:

- https://forarthistory.org.uk
- https://en.wikisource.org/wiki/A_Dictionary_of_Artists_of_the_English_School
- https://en.wikipedia.org/wiki/List_of_Scottish_artists

BAKERS

1841: 37.1 • 1891: 84.1

Bakers have been part of society for many centuries. In medieval times, they often formed local guilds. The Worshipful Company of Bakers (www.bakers.co.uk) dates back to 1155. You may find local archive holdings. Trade directories of the 19th century will list them, of course, and there was an Amalgamated Union of Operative Bakers of England (founded 1861) and the Operative Bakers of Scotland Federal Union (1888).

Useful resources:

- https://wcml.org.uk/the-collection/catalogue/
- MULLER, H.G. 1986. Baking and Bakeries. Shire Publications
- PHILLIPS, Gordon. 1993. 1666 and All That: A History of the Bakers' Company. Granta

BARBERS, HAIRDRESSERS & WIG MAKERS

1841; 10.1 • 1891: 25.4

Barbers began somewhat as part of the medical profession as much as for personal grooming, undertaking surgery and bloodletting as well as cutting hair and shaving. London Metropolitan Archives has records of the Worshipful Company of Barbers. Meanwhile, wigmaking has its own separate heritage, although often associated with barber-surgeons' guilds as barbers frequently took on this task too.

Useful resources:

- https://www.barberscompany.org
- DOBSON, Jessie & WALKER, Robert M. 1979. Barbers and barber-surgeons of London: a history of the Barbers' and Barber-Surgeons' Companies. Barbers' Company
- SHERROW, Victoria. 2006. Encyclopedia of Hair. Greenwood Publishing Group

BARGEMEN, LIGHTERMEN & WATERMEN

1841: 23.6 • 1891: 31.4

Many people have worked on our inland waterways through history, whether on rivers or, from the late 18th century, the canal network. Thames lightermen and watermen formed guilds in the 16th century (see https://watermenscompany.com). Watermen carried fare-paying passengers; lightermen manned flat-bottomed cargo barges. The Canal Museum in London has a checklist for researchers (www.canalmuseum.org.uk/collection/family-history.htm), and the Canal & Rover Trust holds the extensive Waterways Archive.

Useful resources:

- https://collections.canalrivertrust.org.uk
- LEGON, James, 2008. My Ancestors Were Thames Watermen. Society of Genealogists
- WILKES, Sue. 2011. Tracing Your Canal Ancestors. Pen & Sword

BLACKSMITHS

1841: 82.1 • 1891: 125.0

Blacksmiths and farriers (the latter shod horses) played a vital role in supporting a horse-driven economy, but blacksmiths also helped industry and shipbuilding. The Worshipful Company of Blacksmiths (www.blacksmithscompany.co.uk) dates back to at least 1299; the Associated Society of Blacksmiths formed in 1845.

Useful resources:

- https://www.ancestry.co.uk/search/collections/62979
- BAILEY, Jocelyn. 1977. The Village Blacksmith. Shire Publications
- EVANS, Marcia. 1999. The Place of the Rural Blacksmith in Parish Life 1500-1900. Somerset and Dorset FHS

BRASS & BRONZE MANUFACTURERS

1841; 11.8 • 1891: 36.9

Brass (an alloy of copper and zinc) has been in use since Roman times, but before the 17th century it was mostly imported; manufacture of bronze (copper and tin) dates back to beyond 2000BC. A monopoly on brass held by the Royal Mines Company ended in 1689. Thanks to Nehemiah Champion, Bristol became the centre of the brass industry in the 18th century. Brass toys and buttons were both made particularly there and in Birmingham.

Useful resources:

- https://www.familysearch.org/en/wiki/England_Metal_Working_Occupations_A_to_C_-_International_Institute
- EVELEIGH, David J. 1995. Brass and Brassware. Shire Publications
- DAY, Joan & TYLECOTE, R.F. 1991. The Industrial Revolution in Metals. Institute of Metals

BREWERS & MALTSTERS

1841; 17.3 • 1891: 35.4

Brewing has been a key industry in towns and villages everywhere, as beer was safer to drink than water in the past. Hope were introduced around 1400, although breweries as we know them began in the 18th century. Malting is the process of converting barley to malt for use in brewing, and was particularly common in Suffolk, Essex and Hertfordshire. Records are patchy as many breweries came and went, but the Brewery History Society is a good starting point.

Useful resources:

- www.breweryhistory.com
- BARBER, Norman. c1995. A Century of British Brewers 1890-1990. The Brewery History Society
- LOVETT, Maurice. 1981. Brewing and Breweries. Shire Publications

BRICKLAYERS

1841: 39.7 • 1891: 130.5

Bricklayers are distinct from people working in the brickmaking trade. Layers usually served as apprentice, and then often worked in gangs employed by private companies, or they were self-employed. The growth in their numbers was partly because of the Victorian building boom and the rise of the railways. The Operative Society of Bricklayers formed in the early 19th century.

Useful resources:

- https://warwick.ac.uk/services/library/mrc/explorefurther/subject_guides/family_history/brick/
- HAMMOND, Martin. 2001. Bricks and Brickmaking. Shire Publications
- BRUNSKILL, R.W. 1990. Brick Building in Britain. Victor Gollancz

BRICKMAKERS

1841: 17.2 • 1891: 43.7

British brickmaking dates back to Roman times, but the first written records hail from the 16th century, from which period bricks were fired in kilns – they were hand moulded until machinery was developed in the late 19th century. Bedfordshire has been a particular locus for brickmaking. Useful resources are the British Brick Society (www.british-bricksoc.co.uk) and the Old Bricks website (www.brocross.-com/Bricks/Penmorfa/index.htm).

Useful resources:

- http://www.cufley.co.uk/brickmakers/brickmakers-index
- HAMMOND, Martin. 2001. Bricks and Brickmaking. Shire Publications
- DOUGLAS, G. & OGLETHORPE, M. 1993. Brick, Tile and Fireclay Industries in Scotland. The Royal Commission on the Ancient and Historical Monuments of Scotland

BUTCHERS

1841: 46.0 • 1891: 98.9

There are indications of a butcher's hall near Smithfield as early as the 10th century. Butchers were also known as fleshers, and some towns (such as Edinburgh) still have a street named for their fleshmarket. Slaughterhouses needed licences after the Knackers Act of 1786, and details may survive in Quarter Sessions records. The Meat Trades Journal has been published since 1888 and is held by the British Library.

Useful resources:

- www.butchershall.com
- PERREN, Richard. 1978. The Meat Trade in Britain, 1840-1914
- RIXSON, Derrick. 2000. The History of Meat Trading. Nottingham University Press

CABMEN & COACHMEN

1841; 13.4 • 1891: 37.3

Coaches were developed in England in the mid-16th century, initially used only near London until the road surfaces had improved. A century later, a network of stagecoaches had evolved across the country, using inns as staging posts for changing horses. Steel springs made the ride more comfortable from 1754. As well as coachmen themselves, many ostlers and grooms were needed to support this industry. Cab drivers, operating smaller vehicles, formed unions in the 19th century.

Useful resources:

- https://bit.ly/2IxN5Ex
- MAY, Trevor. 1999. Victorian and Edwardian Horse Cabs. Shire Publications
- REYNARDSON, C.T.S.B. 1875. 'Down the Road', or Reminiscences of a Gentleman Coachman

CARPENTERS, JOINERS & CABINET MAKERS

1841: 169.0 • 1891: 305.1

Carpenters, joiners (known for furniture and finishing details) and woodsmiths (the older term) were another trade which tended to form guilds, with the London-based Carpenters' Company dating from 1333, for example. Their trade saw a peak during a housebuilding boom in early modern times, before fires led to more stone buildings, and again in the 19th century when wooden buildings were often required in the colonies. Ships relied on their carpenters too. Cabinet making was a lighter but particularly skilled form of carpentry, with its heyday from Tudor times (for the related trade of upholstering, see https://www.upholders.co.uk).

Useful resources:

- https://warwick.ac.uk/services/library/mrc/research_guides/family_history/carpntr
- BAILEY, Jocelyn. 1975. The Village Wheelwright and Carpenter. Shire Publications
- SPARKES, Ivan G. 1991. Woodland Craftsmen. Shire Publications

CARRIERS & CARTERS

1841: 26.5 • 1891: 170.3

Deliverymen of all kinds were of great importance, long before Amazon Prime. Carriers and carters formed a network between towns and villages, with draymen serving the brewery trade specifically. Old advertisements in trade directories and newspapers can reveal details of these networks.

Useful resources:

- www.britishnewspaperarchive.co.uk
- GERHOLD, Dorian. 1993. Packhorses and wheeled vehicles in England, 1550-1800. Journal of Transport History
- https://www.thecarmen.co.uk

CHARWOMEN

1841: 20.1 • 1891: 104.8

These unsung heroes of society, keeping homes and institutions clean, have not left many clear records. They did not tend to form groups or societies, this being an essentially word-of-mouth occupation. You may find advertisements and listings in directories and newspapers.

Useful resources:

- Memoirs of Victorian Working-Class Women: The Hard Way Up, Florence Boos (Palgrave Macmillan, 2017)
- GREGSON, Nicky & LOWE, Michelle. 1994. Servicing the middle classes : class, gender and waged domestic labour in contemporary Britain
- MAY, Trevor. 1998. The Victorian Domestic Servant. Shire Publications

CHEMISTS, DRUGGISTS & PHARMACISTS

1841; 10.1 • 1891: 21.9

These trades have their origin in apothecaries, who prepared and sold medicines. The London livery company the Worshipful Society of Apothecaries was founded in 1647. Apothecaries could also prescribe medicines, but this changed over time as the practice of physicians developed. The Pharmaceutical Society of Great Britain was founded in 1841, and initiated compulsory registration in 1868. Its archives date to 1842.

Useful resources:

- https://www.rpharms.com/about-us/museum
- JACKSON, W.A. 1996. The Victorian Chemist and Druggist. Shire Publications
- ROOKLEDGE, Keith. 2000. Was Your Ancestor a Chemist? Greentrees

CIVIL SERVANTS

1841; 10.4 • 1891: 76.4

Senior civil servants were listed in almanacs and other directories sine the late 17th century, and the Civil Service Year Book began in 1873. Many appointments were noted in the London Gazette, and the Foreign Office maintained records for civil servants involved in the running of the British Empire. Records of Royal Household staff meanwhile date back to the early 16th century. The National Archives is the main resource, and its holdings include civil service examination records.

Useful resources:

- https://www.nationalarchives.gov.uk/help-with-your-research/research-guides/civil-or-crown-servants/
- PARRIS, Henry. 1960. A Civil Servant's Diary, 1841-6. Public Administration
- LOWE, Rodney. 2011. The Official History of the British Civil Service. Routledge

CLERGYMEN

1841; 20.4 • 1891: 46.1

The Church of England dates back to the 16th century, although the most detailed records date from the 19th century onwards. The Clergy of the Church of England Database (https://theclergydatabase.org.uk) has a huge collection of information from 1540 to 1835; Crockford's Clerical Directory meanwhile began in 1858. The Catholic Family History Society (https://mlfhs.uk/catholic) records have useful information. Consult the John Rylands Library in Manchester (www.library.manchester.ac.uk/rylands/) for Methodist Collections. The rise in clergy numbers in the 19th century was largely boosted by Nonconformist denominations, for which Dr Williams's Library (www.dwl.ac.uk) is a useful starting point.

Useful resources:

- TOWEY, Peter. 2006. My Ancestor Was an Anglican Clergyman. Society of Genealogists.
- RAYMOND, Stuart A. 2017. Tracing Your Nonconformist Ancestors. Pen & Sword (and other titles on C of E and Catholic ancestors)

COACH MAKERS & WHEELWRIGHTS

1841: 37.3 • 1891: 69.9

Coach transport was essential for any form of long-distance travel before the rise of the railways in the 19th century. The Worshipful Company of Coachmakers and Coach Harness Makers was founded in 1677. Coachmakers employed specialist tradesmen such as body-makers, carriage-makers, trimmers and painters to complete the construction and decoration of coaches. Later, these skills were more in demand for making the many kinds of cabs. None of these could have been made without the work of wheelwrights, who also sometimes made carts themselves, and indeed coffins.

Useful resources:

- https://www.coachmakers.co.uk
- MAY, Trevor. 1999. Victorian and Edwardian Horse Cabs. Shire Publications
- HANSON, Harry. 1983. The Coaching Life. Manchester University Press

COAL MINERS

1841: 101.6 • 1891: 517.1

Britain's coal fields have been worked throughout Britain since before the Romans, in Wales and Scotland and even Kent, as well as the coal heartlands of northern England. Coal was the fuel of the Industrial Revolution. Records and archives are extensive – the Coalmining History Resource Centre website no longer exists but is archived (see https://archive.is/www.cmhrc.co.uk) and Ancestry has its database of coal mining accidents 1700-1950.

Useful resources:

- http://www.dmm.org.uk
- TONKS, David. 2014. My Ancestor was a Coalminer. Society of Genealogists.
- ELLIOTT, Brian. 2014. Tracing Your Coalmining Ancestors. Pen & Sword

COMMERCIAL CLERKS

1841: 35 • 1891: 247.3

The white-collar workforce particularly grew in Victorian times, with increased literacy and thriving businesses requiring scribes of various kinds (note the figures above do not include legal and civil service clerks). If you know where your clerking forebear worked, there may be a business archive (found via TNA's Discovery). The National Union of Clerks started in 1890.

Useful resources:

- https://wcml.org.uk/the-collection/catalogue/
- BISHOP, Jennifer. 2016. The Clerk's Tale: Civic Writing in 16th Century London. Past & Present
- ANON. 1957. The 19th Century Banker's Clerk. Three Banks Review

COOPERS

1841; 15.6 • 1891: 17.2

The standard sizes of barrels, made by coopers, were established in 1420. 'White coopers' made these and other vessels and vats, such as milk churns and washtubs; 'dry coopers' made casks for apples, gunpowder and soap; 'wet coopers' for wines, spirits and jams. Coopering continued in Scotland after it has declined in England (see https://www.tradeshouse.org.uk/14-incorporated-crafts/coopers for a guild in Glasgow).

Useful resources:

- www.coopers-hall.co.uk
- KILBY, K. 1977. The Village Cooper. Shire Publications
- ELKINGTON, George. 1933. The Coopers: Company and Craft

COSTERMONGERS & HAWKERS

1841; 14.9 • 1891: 59

Costermongers originally sold 'costard' apples, but by the 19th century the term was used for anyone selling goods from a stall, barrow or cart, while hawkers carried baskets or other, less permanent equipment. Costermongers can be elusive in census records, though they may turn up in court records, and county archives may have details where licences were required. Henry Mayhew's studies of the London poor illuminate some of their lives.

Useful resources:

- London Labour and the London Poor, Henry Mayhew (1851)
- HOGG, Garry. 1974. Market Towns of England. David and Charles
- CHANDLER, Keith. 2005. Gypsies, Hawkers and Other Travellers in the English South Midlands. Romany & Traveller FHS
- LAROON, Marcellus. 1688. The Criers and Hawkers of London

COTTON WORKERS

1841: 217.4 • 1891: 546.0

Cotton manufacture really took off with the invention of spinning machines in the late 18th century – and from then the industry grew astonishingly, powering the British economy and empire. For census takers, the cotton trade posed a problem – in 1841, more job titles were used in this trade in Lancashire than for the whole of the county 10 years earlier. Ancestry has some records of Yorkshire cotton manufacturers. Explore Blackburn's cotton trade at https://www.cottontown.org. Factory records may be in regional archives, and newspapers often reported on accidents in industrial workplaces.

Useful resources:

- https://www.cottontimes.co.uk
- TEASDALE, Vivian. 2009. Tracing Your Textile Ancestors. Pen & Sword
- ASPIN, Chris. 1995. The Cotton Industry. Shire Publications

DOCTORS, DENTISTS & NURSES

1841: 42.4 • 1891: 105.8

In the past, most medical practitioners were barber-surgeons, apothecaries or, less commonly, physicians. The Barber-Surgeons' Company of London was founded in 1540, and maintains an archive, as does the Royal College of Surgeons in Edinburgh for Scotland. The Royal College of Physicians (originally of London; of England from 1858) was founded in 1518. Medical directories and registers proliferated in the mid-19th century (although there are some earlier examples), covering dentists from 1866 (separate Dentists Register from 1888); issues can be found online. The Royal College of Nursing has 19th and 20th century nursing registers.

Useful resources:

- HIGGS, Michelle. 2011. Tracing Your Medical Ancestors. Pen & Sword
- BOURNE, Susan and CHICKEN, Andrew H. 1994. Records of the Medical Professions
- AMSDEN, Peter C. 1999. The Medical Professions and Their Archives. ASAT Productions

DOMESTIC SERVANTS

1841: 985.5 • 1891: 1309.9

By sheer weight of numbers, many of our ancestors, especially female ones, will have had employment in domestic service – even relatively humble middle-class households saw a maid as an essential status symbol. Records can be sparse, but you may find them in surviving household account books, estate archives and the records of charities such as the Girls' Friendly Society and the Salvation Army who wished to help girls keep off the streets.

Useful resources:

- HORN, Pamela. 2009. My Ancestor was in Service. Society of Genealogists
- HIGGS, Michelle.2012. Tracing Your Servant Ancestors. Pen & Sword
- HORN, Pamela. 1975. The Rise and Fall of the Victorian Servant. Gill and MacMillan
- MAY, Trevor. 1998. The Victorian Domestic Servant. Shire Publications

DRAPERS & MERCERS

1841: 27.3 • 1891: 107.0

Drapers and mercers are often lumped together – the former were retailers of cloth, whereas mercery was specifically the trade in silk and linen, originally referring to merchants who imported these rather than shopkeepers. There are strong regional variations in linen drapery – Blackburn, for example, was known for white calico and Somerset for 'bed-tick'. Durham University has records of that city's drapers' guild. The Drapers Record journal was founded in 1881.

Useful resources:

- https://www.thedrapers.co.uk
- https://www.mercers.co.uk
- SUTTON, A.F. 1999. Some Aspects of the Linen Trade, c1130s to 1500. Textile History

ENGINE & MACHINE MAKERS

1841: 8.8 • 1891: 134.9

Here we have trades almost entirely engendered by the Industrial Revolution – machines, boilers and other equipment themselves needed to be designed, manufactured and maintained by machinists and engineers. The Institution of Mechanical Engineers has archives, some of them digitised by Ancestry. The Steam Engine Maker's Society has records dating back to 1835.

Useful resources:

- https://mrc-catalogue.warwick.ac.uk/records/SEM
- JARVIS, Adrian. The Victorian Engineer. Shire Publications
- RAYNER, Derek. Traction Engines and Other Steam Road Engines. Shire Publications

FARMERS & GRAZIERS

1841: 248.5 • 1891: 223.6

Farming dates back to pre-Saxon times, but comes in many guises, from humble Scottish crofters to the landowning minor gentry yeoman farmers of the early modern period. Many records reveal details of the farming life, such as diaries, manorial records, and land records such as tithe commutations (available at TheGenealogist, with maps).

Useful resources:

- https://www.nottingham.ac.uk/manuscriptsandspecialcollections/collectionsindepth/businessrecords/agriculture.aspx
- ARMSTRONG, Alan. 1988. Farmworkers: A Social and Economic History 1770-1980. Batsford
- EVELEIGH, David J. 1991. The Victorian Farmer. Shire Publications.

FISHERFOLK

1841; 10.5 • 1891: 25.2

Fishing, as befits an island nation, dates back to time immemorial. Deep-sea fishing developed in the 18th and 19th centuries, with fishing ports growing to support it, particularly in north-east England and Scotland. The National Archives has crew lists of fishing vessels – see also Merchant Seamen. Fishing vessels were required to be registered from 1786. Fishing apprenticeships were registered from 1835 onwards.

Useful resources:

- WILCOX, Martin. 2009. Fishing & Fishermen: A Guide for Family Historians. Pen & Sword
- WILLS, Simon. 2016. Tracing Your Seafaring Ancestors. Pen & Sword
- TANNER, Matthew. 1996. Scottish Fishing Boats. Shire Publications

GARDENERS

1841: 48.9 • 1891: 179.3

Horticulture has spanning everything from large estates to small municipal allotments, although until the early 20th century, gardens were primarily the preserve of the upper and then the middle classes.

Useful resources:

- https://www.rhs.org.uk/education-learning/libraries-at-rhs
- SYMES, Michael. 2000. A Glossary of Gardens. Shire Publications
- CAMPBELL, Susan. Walled Kitchen Gardens. Shire Publications

GENERAL LABOURERS

1841: 318.5 • 1891: 596

The great uncelebrated masses of the workforce are inevitably hard to find in records. The countless factories spawned by the Industrial Revolution did not necessarily keep good records of their labourers, although county record offices may have company records such as staff wage books and factory logs. Records of unions and similar organisations can be tracked down via the Modern Records Centre in Warwick and the Working Class Movement Library.

Useful resources:

- https://www.wcml.org.uk
- CHILDS, Michael J. 1992. Labour's Apprentices: Working Class Lads in Late Victorian and Edwardian England. Hambledon Press, London
- FOWLER, Simon. 1991. Sources for Labour History. Labour Heritage
- HAMMOND, J.L. & HAMMOND, Barbara. 1917. The Town Labourer. Longman

GLASS MANUFACTURERS

1841: 70 • 1891: 26.2

Glassmaking was probably brought to Britain by the Romans and in medieval times was particularly concentrated in Sussex and Surrey. Glass manufacture remained small-scale in the early industrial era due to heavy taxation between 1745 and 1845, but thereafter there were numerous larger factories, tending to congregate near centres of the coal industry such as the Midlands, Newcastle and southern Scotland.

Useful resources:

- https: / /www.nationalglasscentre.com
- DODSWORTH, Roger. 1996. Glass and Glassmaking. Shire Publications
- HARRIES, John and HICKS, Carola. Discovering Stained Glass. Shire Publications

GROCERS

1841: 50.2 • 1891: 222.9

Grocers, the ancestors of supermarkets, have a heritage dating back to medieval times, experts at preparing goods and food for sale. Newspapers and trade directories are essential research sources.

Useful resources:

- https://www.sainsburyarchive.org.uk
- BUCK, Philip. 1931. Reminiscences of Life in Grocery and Allied Trades. Grocer & Oil Trade Review
- BLACKMAN, Janet. 1967. The Development of the Retail Grocery Trade in the 19th Century. Business History

IRON & STEEL WORKERS

1841: 36.4 • 1891: 202.5

Iron mining and working dates back to ancient times, and in the middle ages, the Sussex Weald was particularly known for iron smelting. Modern steelmaking began in the mid-19th century thanks to the Bessemer process, and in this era Britain was the 'workshop of the world'. Ironworks could be found across the UK, and steelworks were also widespread, though Sheffield came to become most famous for steel and cutlery production. Factory records may be in local archives, with inspection records at TNA.

Useful resources:

- https://www.sheffieldmuseums.org.uk/collections-stories/search/?packageID=69437
- FEARN, Jacqueline. Cast Iron. Shire Publications
- GALE, W.K.V. 1994. Ironworking. Shire Publications

LAWYERS & LEGAL CLERKS

1841; 28.4 • 1891: 49.6

Until 1838, solicitors and attorneys had to be admitted to the courts, which kept records of these admissions. Articles of clerkship date back to the 18th century, and some are held at The National Archives. TNA also has registers of affidavits made by articled clerks in the 18th and 19th centuries. Records of barristers are in KB 4 at TNA, and the Inns of Court hold archives. The Law Lists were published annually from 1775 to 1976. Legal clerks account for half of the figures above – again, see TNA.

Useful resources:

- https://www.lawsociety.org.uk/support-services/library-services/library-access/
- HERBER, M. & BROOKS, B. 2015. My Ancestor was a Lawyer. Society of Genealogists
- WADE, Stephen. 2010. Tracing Your Legal Ancestors. Pen & Sword Family

LEATHER WORKERS

1841: 32.8 • 1891: 56.6

Leather working, even aside from shoemaking (see Shoe & Boot Makers), has historically been an important business, accounting for various distinct trades involved with the making of clothing, containers and other items. At the end of the 18th century leather was the third most important manufactured good after wool and iron. Tanners processed the raw animal hide in a grim trade known for its stench (and thus typically located in poorer areas). Curriers then dressed the hides, giving them an even thickness and oiling and dying them. The different leather trades, such as saddlers, glovemakers and curriers, had separate guilds or livery companies.

Useful resources:

- WALLER, Ian. 2015. My Ancestor Was a Leather Worker. Society of Genealogists
- WATERER, J.W. 1947. Leather in Life, Art and Industry
- CAMERON, E.A. 1998. Leather and Fur: Aspects of Early Medieval Trade and Technology. Archetype

LODGING & BOARDING HOUSE KEEPERS

1841: 7.5 • 1891: 51.2

Taking in lodgers has long been a way for families to supplement their income. As migrant workers flocked to the cities in search of employment, more organised lodging houses became common – Henry Mayhew describes their atmosphere in his studies of the London poor. In the 20th century, the growth of seaside boarding houses reflected a growing class of people taking holidays.

Useful resources:

- The Secret World of the Victorian Lodging House, Joseph O'Neill (Pen & Sword, 2014)
- MEEK, Jeff. 2016. Boarding and Lodging Practices in Early 20th Century Scotland. Continuity and Change
- GORTON, Edna. 1993. London Lodging Houses. Metropolitan

MASONS

1841: 63.8 • 1891: 84.7

Many stonemasons were needed to build the great cathedrals in medieval times; meanwhile there has never been a shortage of need for monumental masons to carve gravestones. The Friendly Society of Operative Stonemasons was formed in 1833.

Useful resources:

- https://wcml.org.uk/the-collection/catalogue/
- https://warwick.ac.uk/services/library/mrc/research_guides/family_history/stone
- HISLOP, Malcolm. Mediaeval Masons. Shire Publications
- STEVENSON, David. 2011. Apprenticeship: Scottish Stonemason's Indentures, 1573-1740. Scottish Archives

MERCHANT SEAMEN

1841: 38.8 • 1891: 107.8

As an island nation, it's unsurprising that many of our ancestors have earned a living transporting goods by sea, and there are many relevant records available such as Lloyd's Register of Shipping, ships' logs, crew lists, and masters' and mates' certificates. Findmypast is particularly strong in this area and TNA has a series of research guides (www.nationalarchives.gov.uk/help-with-your-research/research-guides) about merchant seamen.

Useful resources:

- https://hec.lrfoundation.org.uk/archive-library/lloyds-register-of-ships-online
- WATTS, C.T. & M.J. 2002. My Ancestor Was a Merchant Seaman. Society of Genealogists
- WILLS, Simon. 2012. Tracing Your Merchant Navy Ancestors. Pen & Sword

MESSENGERS & PORTERS

1841: 24.4 • 1891: 179.1

Porters could be found everywhere there was transport or trade, notably docks, markets and of course railway stations. Porters in London were regulated in medieval times and had freeman status. Billingsgate fish market famously had its own licensed porters, from 1699 until 2012. London wine porters belonged to the Vintners Company. Many messengers were children, and this trade has left little in the archives.

Useful resources:

- https://www.nationalarchives.gov.uk/help-with-your-research/research-guides/railway-workers/
- STERN, Walter M. 1960. The Porters of London
- PATON, H.M. 1945. Porters and Tronmen. Old Edinburgh Club

MILLERS

1841: 22.4 • 1891: 22.8

The Domesday Book records that that more than 5,600 water-powered flour mills were in use, and these and windmills were ubiquitous in medieval times. The Industrial Revolution brought steam power and larger-scale production of flour. County record offices may have records of individual mills, and the Mills Archive Trust is an essential resource for both mills and millers.

Useful resources:

- https://www.millsarchive.org
- WATTS, Martin. 1998. Corn Milling. Shire
- WATTS, Martin. 2005. Water and Wind Power. Shire

MILLINERS, DRESSMAKERS & SEAMSTRESSES

1841: 122.8 • 1891: 475.6

Dressmaking as a recognised profession only dates back to the late 17th century, first as mantua-makers and then dressmakers (this term was first used in 1803); many women simply made their own clothes in the past, or have had help from a seamstress. Milliners specialised in hats (a useful resource is https://www.stockport.gov.uk/topic/hat-works). Record offices may have indentures for children from the workhouse apprenticed into these trades.

Useful resources:

- https://www.fashion-era.com/the_seamstress.htm
- WALKLEY, Christina. 1981. The Ghost in the Looking Glass: The Victorian Seamstress
- COLLINS, Jessica. 2013. Jane Holt, Milliner, and Other Women in Business : Apprentices, Freewomen and Mistresses in The Clothworkers Company, 1606-1800. Textile History

NAVY OFFICERS & SEAMEN

1841; 6.2 • 1891: 25.5

The Royal Navy is referred to as the 'senior service' on account of its predating the other armed forces: it can claim to date back to the 9th century. The Royal Marines light infantry force was founded in 1755, but has its origins in the 17th century. Officers have been published in the annual (quarterly from 1841) Navy Lists since 1782; TNA has officers' service registers, campaign medals for WW1 and other service records. The GRO and ScotlandsPeople have naval war death indexes. TNA has ordinary ratings' records after 1873, too; earlier records include ships' muster records and pay books. See also the National Maritime Museum (www.nmm.ac.uk).

Useful resources:

- TNA guides at https://bit.ly/2s1OMPp
- WALLER, Ian. 2014. My Ancestor Was in the Royal Navy. Society of Genealogists
- DIVALL, Ken. 2008. My Ancestor Was a Royal Marine. Society of Genealogists
- FOWLER, Simon. 2011. Tracing Your Naval Ancestors. Pen & Sword

PLASTERERS & WHITEWASHERS

1841; 11.8 • 1891: 29.4

Plasterers traditionally worked with lime, sand and water, applying plaster to thin strips of wood known as laths to provide a finishing layer to walls and ceilings in construction. Their trade was hazardous, with lung conditions particularly common. The first national union, the National Association of Operative Plasterers, was founded in 1860.

Useful resources:

- https://warwick.ac.uk/services/library/mrc/research_guides/family_history/plaster
- VIVIAN-NEAL, A.W. 1940. A Somerset Plasterer of the 17th Century. Notes & Queries for Somerset & Dorset
- LAING, Alastair. 1986. Foreign Decorators and Plasterers in England, in HIND, C. (ed) The Rococo in England. Victoria & Albert Museum

PLUMBERS, DECORATORS & GLAZIERS

1841: 44.0 • 1891: 170.6

Today we separate the trades of plumbing, painting and decorating, and glazing, but in the past the boundaries were blurred – and in any case plumbing referred more generally to the casting of lead. This could have been for guttering, water cisterns, statuary and even coffins as well as simple pipe work. The Victorian housebuilding boom clearly boosted all of these trades. There is a Worshipful Company of Plumbers with records going back to 1365. The Amalgamated Society of House Decorators and Painters has registration books from 1873-1900.

Useful resources:

- https://warwick.ac.uk/services/library/mrc/research_guides/family_history/ashdp
- LAMB, H.A.J. 1946. Sanitation of Yesterday and Today: Plumbing and Heating of the Past and Present. Architectural Design & Construction
- CHAMPNESS, W. H. 1951. Short History of the Worshipful Company of Plumbers

POLICE

1841: 13.5 • 1891: 39.9

Although every parish had its constable in the past, originally appointed by the manor and later by parish authorities, the formal police force only began slowly in the mid-18th century, evolving from the Bow Street Runners into the Metropolitan Police (although technically the City of Glasgow Police was founded earlier, in 1800). Most modern police forces, and their records, date from the mid-19th century.

Useful resources:

- SHERMAN, Antony. 2000. My Ancestor was a Policeman. Society of Genealogists
- WADE, Stephen. 2009. Tracing Your Police Ancestors. Pen & Sword
- FOUNTAIN, Michael. 1996. My Ancestor was a Policeman. Metropolitan

POTTERY MAKERS (EARTHENWARE/CHINA/PORCELAIN)

1841: 23.8 • 1891: 56.6

Pottery making dates back at least to the Stone Age. English Delftware in the 16th century was associated with Liverpool, Bristol and Wincanton, with similar ware hailing from Glasgow and Dublin. Potters have worked across the isles, but the industrialisation of pottery in the late 18th century focused most notably in the 'Potteries' area around Stoke-on-Trent, fuelled by this region's abundance of clay, coal and water. For Stoke-based resources, see https://www.thepotteries.org/pottery.htm. For Scotland, turn to the Scottish Pottery Society (www.scottishpotterysociety.co.uk).

Useful resources:

- https://wcml.org.uk/the-collection/catalogue/
- SEKERS, David. 1994. The Potteries. Shire Publications
- DRAPER, Jo. Post-Mediaeval Pottery. Shire Publications
- MORLAND, Bill. 1985. Portrait of the Potteries. Robert Hale

PRINTERS & BOOKBINDERS

1841: 21.8 • 1891: 86.5

Before the 15th century invention of the printing press, printing was done with wood blocks; movable type revolutionised this, but was still a skilled and painstaking process. London was the nexus of the printing trade, but by the turn of the 19th century printers could be found in most towns, growing with the rise of newspapers. The Modern Records Centre has records of the many printing and bookbinding unions.

Useful resources:

- RAMSDEN, Charles. 1954. Bookbinders of the United Kingdom (plus London volume) 1780-1840. Batsford
- BROWN, Philip. 1982.London Publishers and Printers 1800-1870. British Library
- DUFF, E. Gordon. 1905. A Century of the English Book Trades. Bibliographical Society
- GREEN, Linda. 1996. Printers and Papermakers. Greentrees
- HUDSON, Graham. 1996. The Victorian Printer

PUBLICANS & HOTEL KEEPERS

1841: 52.9 • 1891: 78

Society's ever-fluctuating relationship with alcohol (once essential when water wasn't safe to drink) and consequent periods of regulation and licensing means that records of publicans and related trades are often abundant. www.pubhistorysociety.co.uk has lots of information, as does Simon Fowler's book Researching Brewery and Publican Ancestors.

Useful resources:

- http://www.sfowler.force9.co.uk/page_12.htm
- WITTICH, John. Discovering London's Inns and Taverns. Shire Publications
- BURKE, Thomas. 1947. The English Inn. Country Books
- HARE, John. 2013. Inns, Innkeepers and the Society of Later Medieval England, 1350-1600. Journal of Medieval History

QUARRIERS

1841; 14.8 • 1891: 52.7

Quarrying goes back to ancient times. Cornwall and Devon have the most important deposits of china clay outside China itself. Flint was excavated particularly from the South and North Downs. Cornwall, Devon and northern Scotland are known for their granite; Wales for its slate. See also Masons.

Useful resources:

- https://warwick.ac.uk/services/library/mrc/research_guides/family_history/stone
- STANIER, Peter. 2000. Quarries and Quarrying. Shire Publications
- THOMAS, I. & ROBERTS, W.O. 2014. Quarry Industry in Wales: A History. National Stone Centre

RAILWAY WORKERS

1841: 19.2 • 1891: 259.5

The figures above reflect the birth of the railway in the 1840s – and how the industry exploded in the decades that followed. The railways created countless jobs, from navvies to clerks, porters to engine drivers, firemen to insurers. Some railway company records can be found online, and the larger companies' staff records are at TNA.

Useful resources:

- HARDY, Frank. 2014. My Ancestor Was a Railway Worker. Society of Genealogists
- DRUMMOND, Di. 2010. Tracing Your Railway Ancestors. Pen & Sword
- HAWKINGS, David. 1995. Railway Ancestors: A Guide to Staff Records. Alan Sutton
- MAY, Trevor. 2000. The Victorian Railway Worker. Shire Publications

SHIP & BOAT BUILDERS

1841: 19.9 • 1891: 62.7

Ships and boats were traditionally built in wood until the second half of the 19th century, when iron and steel were also used. The trade involved many specialist crafts, from joiners and sawyers initially, to engine and boiler makers and fitters latterly. The Working Class Movement Library has useful resources in its catalogue at https://wcml.org.uk/the-collection/catalogue/. The Associated Society of Shipwrights was founded in 1882.

Useful resources:

- https://bit.ly/2IDYC1d
- BURTON, Antony. 2010. Tracing Your Shipbuilding Ancestors. Pen & Sword
- STAMMERS, M.K. Historic Ships. Shire Publications
- STAMMERS, M.K. Steamboats. Shire Publications

SHOE & BOOT MAKERS

1841: 190.8 • 1891: 248.7

Most villages would have had a shoemaker or cobbler, and towns such as Northampton, Street, Norwich and Leicester were all particularly known for their footwear connections. Cordwainers were often shoemakers but might also make other leather goods. Shoe and boot making was mechanised from the 1850s.

Useful resources:

- https://www.northamptonshirebootandshoe.org.uk
- SWANN, June. 1986. Shoemaking. Shire Publications
- HATLEY, V.A. & RAJCZONEK, J. Shoemakers in Northamptonshire, 1762-1911

SHOPKEEPERS (GENERAL)

1841: 25.3 • 1891: 53.6

Shops began as market stalls or 'booths' in medieval times, often congregating into groups (hence street names such as Cornmarket, Fishmarket, etc, and the Shambles indicating where butchers could be found). Trade directories are an obvious place to track down shopkeeping ancestors by county; local archives may have the records of specific, larger businesses. Bankruptcy notices can be traced in the London, Edinburgh, Dublin and Belfast Gazettes. Many shops in the 19th and 20th centuries have advertised in local newspapers.

Useful resources:

- https://le.ac.uk/library/special-collections/explore/historical-directories
- MUI, L.H. & MUI, H.-C. 1989. Shops and Shopkeeping in 18th Century England
- BENSON, J. & UGOLINI, L. 2002. A Nation of Shopkeepers: Retailing in Britain, 1550-2000. I.B. Tauris

SILK, LACE & HOSIERY MANUFACTURERS

1841: 97.2 • 1891: 97.0

Silk thread has always had to be imported to Britain because of the cold climate, but silk goods have been made here with it since medieval times. Staffordshire and Cheshire were home to many silk throwsters, and the Huguenot influx in the late 16th and 17th centuries created silk weaving centres in Canterbury, Norwich, London's Spitalfields and elsewhere. Silk had its heyday in the 19th century before import taxes were relaxed in 1860. Flemish and Huguenot refugees also boosted the lace industry, which has traditionally had its heart in Nottinghamshire (see www.nottinghamindustrialmuseum.org.uk), Derbyshire and Leicestershire. For information about framework knitting, see www.frameworkknittersmuseum.org.uk.

Useful resources:

- TEASDALE, Vivian. 2009. Tracing Your Textile Ancestors. Pen & Sword
- BUSH, Sarah. 1987. The Silk Industry. Shire Publications

STRAW PLAITING

1841: 19.2 • 1891: 18.4

Straw has been important for many products, from mattresses to thatched roofs, furniture to archery targets. Since the 17th century, straw plaiting has been particularly associated with Bedfordshire (and Buckinghamshire, Berkshire, Essex and Hertfordshire to a lesser extent), where straw hats were traditionally made in small cottage industries and, later, larger factories.

Useful resources:

- INWARDS, Harry. 1922. Straw Hats, Their History and Manufacture
- STANIFORTH, Arthur. 1981.Straw and Straw Craftsmen. Shire Publications
- NICHOLS, M.J. 1996. Straw Plaiting and the Straw Hat Industry in Britain. Costume

TAILORS & CLOTHIERS

1841: 120.0 • 1891: 208.7

Tailors tended to be based in towns, where there was more business, though some were journeymen travelling from one community to another to fix people's clothes. Their work was highly skilled, but was eventually stitched up by the mass production facilitated by mechanised textile manufacture.

Useful resources:

- https://wcml.org.uk/the-collection/catalogue/
- ALDRICH, W. 2000. Tailors' Cutting Manuals and Growing Provision of Popular Clothing, 1770-1870. Textile History
- THURSFIELD, S. 2012. The Medieval Tailor's Assistant: Making Common Garments 1200-1500. Ruth Bean.

TEACHERS & LECTURERS

1841: 52.0 • 1891: 212.4

Records of teachers can be found associated with the institutions which trained them, such as the Royal College of Preceptors or the National Society for Promoting the Education of the Poor (see https://microform.digital/boa/collections/76/volumes/534/national-society-for-promoting-the-education-of-the-poor-1812-1900); and also with records of the schools where they taught. TheGenealogist has many school and university registers and teacher-specific records, for example. Findmypast has school admission registers and teachers' registration records.

Useful resources:

- https://www.nationalarchives.gov.uk/help-with-your-research/research-guides/teacher-training/
- MAY, Trevor. 1996-1. The Victorian Schoolroom. Shire Publications
- CURTIS, S.J. 1965. History of education in Great Britain. University Tutorial Press

WASHERWOMEN & LAUNDRY WORKERS

1841: 47.5 • 1891: 192.1

Before the advent of the washing machine in the mid-20th century, there was plenty of work for laundry workers, who were mostly female – the trade often kept them from the workhouse. A mid-19th century report in London may be partly responsible for the pejorative association with 'scrubbers' and prostitution, more likely to be a reflection of poverty than moral turpitude.

Useful resources:

- MALCOLMSON, Patricia E. 1986. English Laundresses: A Social History, 1850-1930. University of Illinois Press
- MALCOLMSON, Patricia E. 1981. Laundresses and the Laundry Trade in Victorian England. Victorian Studies
- GLASSE, H. 1760. The Servant's Directory, or Housekeeper's Companion

WATCH, CLOCK & TOY MAKERS

1841; 13.5 • 1891: 23.9

Watch and clock making date back to the Middle Ages, but took off in the 18th century with the improvement in precision, both for accuracy and miniaturisation. London was the centre of the trade in the 18th and 19th centuries, with many craftsmen having Huguenot or German origins. The Worshipful Company of Clockmakers dates back to 1631. Some workers in these trades also made clockwork toys. (For toys, see https://www.vam.ac.uk/moc.)

Useful resources:

- https://www.sciencemuseum.org.uk/see-and-do/clockmakers-museum
- WEISS, Leonard. 1982. Watchmaking in England 1760-1820. Robert Hale
- BRITTEN, F.J. 1884. Watch and Clockmakers' Handbook, Dictionary and Guide
- BRITTEN, F.J. 1932. Old Clocks and Watches and Their Makers. S.R. Publishers
- SCHROEDER, Joseph J. 1971. The Wonderful World of Toys, Games and Dolls 1860-1930

WEAVERS & SPINNERS

1841: 99.0 • 1891: 9.4

The census figures for weavers speak for themselves – after mechanisation, the trade became mostly redundant, and it's hardly surprising this led to the anger of the Luddites and machine breakers. In earlier times, Huguenot immigrants were noted for weaving. The Worshipful Company of Weavers is London's oldest surviving livery company. There are many textile museums revealing their trade – see https://www.weaverstriangle.co.uk for example.

Useful resources:

- https://www.huguenotsociety.org.uk/library-and-archive.html
- BENSON, Anna & WARBURTON, Neil. 1995. Looms and Weaving. Shire Publications
- LEADBETTER, Eliza. Spinning and Spinning Wheels. Shire Publications

WOOLLEN WORKERS

1841: 88.7 • 1891: 122.9

Before the dominance of cotton, wool was the textile which underpinned many British towns' economies, especially in areas such as the Cotswolds. Medieval monasteries pioneered sheep farming and the wool trade, then guilds sprang up. Until industrialisation created woollen mills, wool spinning, weaving and dyeing were mostly domestic occupations.

Useful resources:

- https://museum.wales/wool
- TEASDALE, Vivian. 2009. Tracing Your Textile Ancestors. Pen & Sword
- ASPIN, Chris. 1982. The Woollen Industry. Shire Publications

GENERAL BIBLIOGRAPHY

ANON. 1827. The Book of English Trades and Library of Useful Arts. Available at https://archive.org/details/bookofenglishtra00unse

BOOTH, Charles. 1881. Occupations of the People of the United Kingdom 1801-81. Reprinted as Chapter 1 in ROUTH, Guy. 1987. Occupations of the People of Great Britain. MacMillan Press, London. FHL book 942 U2rgo.

BROWN, Jonathan. 2011. Tracing Your Rural Ancestors. Pen & Sword

BROWN, L.M. & CHRISTIE, I.R. 1977. Bibliography of British History, 1789-1851. Oxford University Press

BURLISON, Robert. 2009. Tracing Your Pauper Ancestors. Pen & Sword

CRAIL, Mark. 2009. Tracing Your Labour Movement Ancestors. Pen & Sword

CULLING, Joyce. 1999. Occupations: A Preliminary List. FFHS Publications

EMM, Adele. 2015. Tracing Your Trade and Craftsman Ancestors. Pen & Sword

JEWELL, Andrew. 1968. Crafts, Trades and Industries: A Book List for Local Historians. National Council of Social Service

LANSDELL, Avril. 1984-1. Occupational Costume and Working Clothes 1776-1976. Shire Publications.

RAYMOND, Stuart A. 1996. Occupational Sources for Genealogists. FFHS Publications

RAYMOND, Stuart A. 2011. Trades and Professions: The Family Historian's Guide. The Family History Partnership

RAYMOND, Stuart A. 2014. My Ancestor was an Apprentice. Society of Genealogists

ROUTH, Guy. 1987. Occupations of the People of Great Britain. Palgrave Macmillan Press

WILLIAMS-MITCHELL, C. 1982. Dressed for the Job. The story of occupational costume. Blandford

www.ingramcontent.com/pod-product-compliance
Ingram Content Group UK Ltd.
Pitfield, Milton Keynes, MK11 3LW, UK
UKHW040012200726
13854UKWH00001B/156